Real Estate Lead Generation:

The Quick and Easy Way to Generate Real Estate Leads

By Brent Driscoll

More books by Brent Driscoll:

Wholesaling Real Estate: A Beginners Guide

Becoming a Real Estate Agent: A Comprehensive Guide on How to Become a Real Estate Agent

Flipping Houses for Profit: A Comprehensive Guide on How to Flip Houses for Maximum ROI

Rental Property Investing for the Rest of Us: The Beginners Guide to Successful Rental Property Investing

Table of Contents

Chapter 1 - Why Lead Generation is an Essential Business Practice 6
   Customers Hate Marketing – Or Do They? 6
   How to Use Leads 7

Chapter 2   - .... The Use of the Internet 8
   Part 1: Your Company Website 8
      How to Get Their Contact Information 8
      Offer Your Readers Something of Value 10
   Part 2 – Use Social Media to Build Trust 12
      How to Build Trust with Social Media 13
      How to Generate Real Leads from Social Media 14
      How to Promote Your Social Media 15
   Part 3 – Use Forums to Build Your Reputation 15
   Part 4 – Use Google Maps to Direct Interest to You 16
   Part 5 – Generate Leads through Email 17
   Part 6 - Maximize the Internet to Channel Leads to Your Website . 18

Chapter 3   - .... The Use of Advertising Media 19
   Part 1 – Phone Numbers 19
   Part 2 – Answer Systems 20

Part 3 – Classified Ads 20

Part 3 – Targeted Mailing Lists 21

Part 4 – Referrals 21

Chapter 4 – The Use of Personal Contact 23

Part 1 – Open Houses 23

    Sign-In Sheets 24

    The Printed Material 25

    The Conversation 25

Part 2 – Work Your Farm 27

Part 3 – Attend Real Estate Support Groups 28

Part 4 – Participate in Community Events 28

Part 5 – Telemarketing the Good Way 29

Chapter 5 – How to Convert Your Leads into Clients 31

Use Software to Manage Your Leads 31

Create a System 34

Get a VA to Help 35

Chapter 6 – 10 Tips to Effectively Generate Leads 37

Tip #1 – Create a System to Generate Leads 38

Tip #2 – Do Not Annoy Potential Clients 38

Tip #3 – Provide a Product or Service in Exchange for a Lead 38

Tip #4 – Generate Leads Everyday 39

Tip #5 – Follow up on Each and Every Lead 39

Tip #6 – Maximize Your Leads through Customer Relationship Management (CRM) Software 39

Tip #7 – Build an Online Presence with Local Residents 39

Tip #8 – Generate Leads by Giving Back to the Community 40
Tip #9 – Do not Forget to Use Direct Mail Marketing..................40
Tip #10 – Stick to Your System...40

Chapter 1 - Why Lead Generation is an Essential Business Practice

A successful real estate business is built on the execution of a redundant cycle. This cycle starts with generating leads, converting them to clients and then completing the transaction. The more this cycle is completed, the more business you will generate.

Without this on-going cycle, your business will spit and sputter like an old Ford that is missing a spark plug. Just one failed step and the whole business will be effected.

Perhaps the most critical step in this system is lead generation. Like the pistons in a vehicle, it powers the rest of the engine and creates momentum. If you do not continue to generate leads, then as you complete a transaction you will lose forward momentum.

There are plenty of ways to generate a prospect or potential customer. We are going to analyze all of the most common lead generation methods that successful real estate agents are using. The goal here is to obtain email addresses, phone numbers and or mailing addresses in order to cultivate their interest and hopefully turn them from a prospect into a paying customer.

Customers Hate Marketing – Or Do They?

You have come home from a stressful day at the office. You finally sit down to a nice home cooked meal with your family... and then the phone rings. You answer the phone only to realize there is a telemarketer on the other line. Your blood pressure skyrockets as you brusquely end the conversation.

In general, we hate to be marketed to. We do not like products being pushed at us or our family. We know they are trying to make money off of us and it makes us distrust them. Even if the product satisfies a need, if the presentation is too "in your face," we will look elsewhere.

Lead generation is the end product of marketing and therefore it is common for inexperienced agents to have misgivings and even hold off from executing an effective lead generation system for fear of being to pushy.

Rather than looking at lead generation as marketing to a prospect, think of it as providing a service for someone in need. Consumers are more educated now than in any other time in history. They are constantly looking for information and advice. If they can find answers to their questions, they are more likely to do business with the source of the advice.

That means that if you can help consumers, advise buyers and mentor investors, you can build a rapport of trust. It is trust that converts prospects into customers.

How to Use Leads

There are three main uses for lead generation:

- Create Interest
- Education
- Marketing

Lead generation should create an interest in your product or service. It is their response to the marketing that stirs interest which then creates a lead. When you answer a question or prepare articles that educate a prospect, their desire to obtain more information will encourage them to provide contact information generating another lead.

Generate Leads Through...

Chapter 2 — The Use of the Internet

Using the internet is currently perhaps the most widely used method of lead generation – and one of the most effective. There are several avenues within the internet in which you can capitalize on.

This chapter is going to analyze each of those methods and show you how to tweak your website, pull in genuine interest, generate leads by strengthening your reputation and lots more.

Part 1: Your Company Website

Hundreds of millions of dollars are spent annually by companies attempting to drive interest to their website. Unfortunately hits alone do not generate leads. The goal of internet advertising is to convert those nameless hits into genuine leads.

How to Get Their Contact Information

If your potential customer likes what they read and would like to either receive more information or receive some sort of personal contact, you need to make it easy for them to provide their information. Do not make a prospect hunt around for your contact information. Make it super easy for them to provide their follow-up information. Consider these methods:

- The Side Bar Opt-In. This is the quiet, non-invasive "Share your email to get something" box which is usually found on the right hand side of the home or leading page of a website.

- **Pop Up or Slide-In Box:** These boxes pop-up upon entry or exit. They can also be timed to pop-up as well. These boxes often offer access to private webpages or blogs, an eBook, free quote or consultation or a limit time offer. If you want these boxes to work, do not have them pop up as soon as the page is accessed. Readers have come to that page for a purpose (such as to read an article that interests them). They do not want to give you any information yet, they just met you. Instead time the box to appear after it would take a typical reader time to read 75% of the article. Your response rate will be much higher.

- **Hello Bar** – This is a lead capture bar found at the top of the screen that advertises more content or a webinar. When it is clicked on, it asks for an email address in exchange for the promised content.

- **Footer Bar** – Though similar to the Hello Bar, this widget appears at the bottom of a page or at the end of a blog asking for the visitor to subscribe to receive regular content.

- **Welcome Gate** – This page asks for an email address before granting access to the site. A visitor can click past it but many, not realizing it, will enter their email. This method often turns away prospects and should be used on a limited basis.

These are an excellent tool to ask for referrals. You can even "bribe" your reader for a referral by offering them a bonus if their referral ends up doing business with you. Consider a gift card to a local business as a suitable bribe.

We have to keep in mind that our visitors are wise to scams and tend to be skeptical of giving out their email or other contact information. They are afraid that they will receive the middle-of-dinner-telemarketing-phone call or the daily email that fills up their inbox. So offer something of value. Ask for contact information after you have engaged them.

Offer Your Readers Something of Value

You need to provide something that will make them *want* to give you their email address. If you are providing information or assistance of value, then your visitors will recognize the quality and you can expect 10% of your hits to leave their email address. Here are some ideas of content that readers will exchange their email address for:

- **Content Upgrade** – If you have premium content, exchange access to it for an email address. Lead pages are good for this.

- **Membership** – Membership needs to have benefits. A monthly newsletter is not as appealing as it used to be. Instead consider offering quarterly comparative market analysis (CMA) reports, industry studies or priority emails of new listings and solds.

- **Free Consultation or Quotes** – Though this will take some extra time on your part to fulfill, this can be time well spent. It can be an excellent way to quickly convert a prospect into a client.

- **EBooks and Tip Guides** – A landing page that promotes an eBook that captures the interest of your reader can be a compelling reason to give up their email address. Subjects for eBooks can include:
    - First Time Buyer's Handbook
    - Investment Secrets
    - Remodeling Projects That Pay Off

- Simple Steps to Quickly Sell Your House
- 10 Mistakes Buyers Make
- How to Finance Your Real Estate Purchase

- **Online Chat/Help Desk** – This is a great way to capitalize on any questions or concerns they may have. Combining an online chat with a pop-up box can quickly grab attention.

- **Free Online Course** – Consumers love getting information for free and if they can get training for free then all the better. This will give your potential customers the opportunity to learn from you over a period of time. By the time the last course is completed, you could have assembled plenty of information from your contact off of surveys and other data gathering participation. Some ideas for an online course could include:
    - How to sell Your House in 30 Days
    - How to Buy a House in 30 Days
    - How to Flip a House in 180 Days
    - How to Use Real Estate to Finance Retirement

- **Webinar** – Do not just stream a video of yourself talking about a service you offer. They can find that on YouTube. Instead, offer a question and answer session which will allow you to personally connect with your leads. This is an excellent way to build a solid reputation as an industry professional and it also establishes trust and builds a relationship with these participants.

- Online Offer – You will need to provide a good reason for these prospects to buy your offer. It could be of limited availability or answer a hot question that is leading the news. Online offers that attract attention include:
    - How to Use Your Retirement Account to Buy Real Estate
    - Creative Ways to Finance Your Property Purchase
    - How to Get and Keep Great Tenants

- Blogs – A blog is becoming an essential part of a website. Visitors expect to see one. But do not use it to sell yourself or even your services. Its main purpose is to provide information. If your blog provides fresh content that is of real use to your readers, they will be willing to exchange their email address to receive notifications of new articles.

- Videos – Web surfers have an appetite for graphical content. Viewers, on the average, spend twice as much time on pages that have videos. Since real estate agents are in the service business, presenting a video of yourself is a great way to welcome leads. Videos engage the visitor and are easy to share. At the end of the video, offer the next in the series if they agree to opt-in. Rather than promoting your company or services with pay-per-click ads, consider promoting your video. The response will be dramatic.

Part 2 – Use Social Media to Build Trust

Social media includes sites such as Twitter, YouTube, Google+, Facebook and LinkedIn. The main purpose of social media is not about advertising but about connecting, sharing and exchanging ideas. This is an important point to remember for businesses.

Do not think of social media as a marketing or promotional tool. Instead, focus on providing a service, sharing tips and keeping in contact with your past, present and future clients. Nothing will turn off a social media participant as blatant business promotion. It can even get you blacklisted by the site itself. Spam is even worse. Uninvited self-promotion is the HIV of the internet. It may not directly affect others but it will kill your business reputation.

When it comes to direct sales generation, social media is not the most effective method, but it is an excellent tool for building trust - and trust is a fundamental cornerstone of the real estate industry. If your clients trust you they will tell others and generate leads for you. If you provide valuable information, tips and services then when it comes time for visitors to choose an agent, they will most often choose the one they have built a relationship with over social media.

How to Build Trust with Social Media

Rather than self-promotion, concentrate on participation. Look at this as an opportunity to mentor. If you can give evidence of knowing your market and being an expert in your field, then local readers are going to remember that when they drive-by and see your face on a yard sign. When it comes time for them to buy or sell their house, who do you think they will call? The person they know and trust or a name off a yellow page ad or Google search? Think of social media as an extension of your physical marketing. Do not just aimlessly interact, instead focus on participants from your market area.

To build trust, first create engaging content on your page. Post or tweet valuable content. This could be new listings or solds. But do not stop there. How about posting local events and community activities? Even local business promotions, sales and specials can keep your followers coming back to see what is new. Share tips and advice on a daily basis and feel free to re-share old content with different audiences within a few weeks. Make sure you actively promote any products or videos that are offered on your website. Videos have an excellent click-through response and work very well to direct social media traffic to your website. Just make sure your videos teach or provide a service rather than being simply promotional.

Take the time to interact within social media. Don't just hang out on your page. When you stay "home," you are only interacting with existing clients and we want to focus on generating new clients. To do this, you will need to leave the comfort of your Facebook page and start interacting with strangers.

Comment on other posts – especially posts that are coming out of your physical market area. Feel free to share their appropriate content with others. Work to build followers and contacts. Answer their questions. Share appropriate advice (without giving the feeling like you are pushing your services). Comment on other people's posts, videos, tweets and blog articles. Just relax and join a conversation.

How to Generate Real Leads from Social Media

If you have correctly set up your account, every time you post – either on your page or someone else's – there is a link back to your website. Not only does this provide a reader with the chance to become a genuine lead, but it will build your website ranking as well.

When setting up your profile, design it in a way that invites people to connect with you. If there is a summary statement, take the time to design a spot on statement that grabs their attention and makes them want to see your website - since that is where the conversion will take place. (*Have you implemented Part 1 yet?*) Make sure the link to your website address works correctly. You should design leading pages that are directly focused on leads generated from social media sites and then put that link in the profile rather than directing them to your home page.

Another way to build trust is to link up with other industry professionals. Professional social media sites such as Google+ and LinkedIn have been designed for that purpose. Look to create a network with appraisers, attorneys, title agencies, home inspectors and contractors that are from your market area. Interact with them. Share their posts on your site. Give out advice when asked. Promote their services, where appropriate. When they find out, they will do the same for you.

Within Facebook, head over to the Facebook Insights tab to see when your fans are online. This will determine when the most effective time to post. In addition, take advantage of Google analytics to see your conversion rates. This will help you to see which social media site is generating the most clicks to your site and where they go after they arrive. This will help you know where to place conversion boxes (*See Part 1.*)

How to Promote Your Social Media
Your printed and online advertising should work in harmony with your social media. Just as your social media account links back to your website, make sure that your website promotes your social media accounts. This can be as simple as including a linked icon on your home page. In addition, the icons for your social media sites should be found on all of your marketing materials.

It is a dream come true if a social media post or a blog article goes viral. You can help to make that possible by creating the opportunity. After each blog, post, tweet or Thank You page include a "Share" or retweet button. The share button is much more effective than a simple "Like" which promotes very little. Help your readers promote your site for you.

Over the long-term, social media can be frustrating. It may seem that very few of your converted leads will be coming from social media, but do not underestimate the effect your participation has had on their choice of a real estate agent. The long-term value that you provide on social media will have results. Make sure that you are consistently posting 2-3 times a day. If you lack the time to effectively manage social media, hire an online cheap virtual assistant through sites like Upwork.com.

Part 3 – Use Forums to Build Your Reputation
Though social media is a necessary part of business promotion, I have found that participating in real estate related forums are even more effective. It is an easy way to build a reputation for being an expert in your field. Some of the top real estate forums include:

- Trulia "Voices"
- Zillow "Advice"
- BiggerPockets

Here readers come to ask questions. They are looking for advice. These are all potential clients and if you can interact with ones within your market area all the better. Both Trulia and Zillow allow you to search for forum posts based on a geographical area. Once these accounts are setup properly, each post you make will include your logo and a link back to your website.

Again, make sure that you are answering their question and not blatantly promoting yourself or your website. Most sites allow you to post links within your comment. Including a link to a government website that will answer a question about zoning is good. Posting a link about your new blog article that has nothing to do with the question is bad and can get you blacklisted. Spamming forums will do more to harm your internet reputation than if you never participated in the first place.

Regularly - as in daily - posting on forums is an effective way to build search engine ranking. It also is a great tool for referrals. This is an area that each real estate professional should not overlook. With sites like BiggerPockets, make sure you check back on the threads where you posted just in case some follow up is needed.

Part 4 – Use Google Maps to Direct Interest to You

Though Google+ did not turn out to be the top social media site that Google was hoping for, Google maps is still a powerful search tool, as is Yahoo's and Bing's map features. What is more, once you set up an account, you have control over what is seen by consumers.

Stop reading for just a moment and go find out what potential clients see about you when they do a general search. Start with a Google search. Type in "real estate agents <your town name>." Where are you in the list? Are you in the top 5 or at least the top 10?

If you want to rank higher than you may need to complete your maps listing. Verify it. Include as much data as allowed. Include pictures, links to your website, phone numbers, address etc. The more information the better. Verified and up-to-date sites will rank higher. Now go and do the same thing in Yahoo and Bing.

When buyers and sellers start looking for an agent they will often do a search and choose the best looking listing that is in close proximity to their home. If you have taken the time to get your search engine ranking up there, then you very well could be their top choice – or at least they will visit your website giving you the opportunity to get a genuine lead.

Part 5 – Generate Leads through Email

Back in the day, advertising was done through bulk mail. You would purchase a mailing list and then flood them with advertising material. Though bulk mailing is still available, many businesses have turned their attention to a far cheaper method – email.

You can manually send email messages or you can use online tools to do that for you. Some of the top auto responders are [Mailchimp](), [Aweber](), [iContact](), and [Get Responses](). These auto responders receive your leads and then broadcast emails to your lead list.

Autoresponders need to be used with caution, however. Unless your emails contain something of value to the reader, they can easily be discarded and classified as spam. Once labeled as such, your emails will automatically be directed to their trash can and never to be seen or read again.

Think of email lead generation as a way to build and maintain relationships. It is all about staying in touch with people. Be personal. Create specific landing pages on your website that complements your emails.

Part 6 - Maximize the Internet to Channel Leads to Your Website

The internet is an extremely powerful lead generation tool. According to the National Association of Realtors, 88% of home buyers use online websites to search for homes. If you are not maximizing your exposure and interaction within the internet, you are losing leads – daily leads.

Make sure that you are implementing each of these four steps so that they will work together to farm leads. Concentrate on creating an effective website that encourages visitors to leave contact information. Make it easy for them. Provide items of value and advice that builds trust.

Trust is the foundation that converts leads into clients

.

Generate Leads Through...

Chapter 3 – The Use of Advertising Media

Though the internet has become a dominant advertising medium to generate leads, conversions and customers, you should not discount the value of more traditional forms of advertising media. This chapter is going to discuss which methods are yielding solid leads. We will also share some tricks of the trade.

Part 1 – Phone Numbers

Yes, I know of course you have a business number already. But have you ever thought about using phone numbers as a way to measure conversion? You are already including a phone number on each advertisement, but what if you used a different number for your postcards, a different one for your emails and a next one for your website? You would then instantly know which advertising method is generating the most leads.

That does not mean that you need to install multiple phone lines, rather have them come through the internet. In order to create a more believable first impression, however, use local numbers rather than 1-800. In fact, you can get local numbers for each advertising region if you want to measure response over a greater area.

There is another facet to using phone numbers that will actually help to generate more solid leads. Your advertising method generated interest, the phone call gives you a solid lead but now you want to convert that lead as fast as possible. That can be done by using a voice-mail system.

Part 2 – Answer Systems

The kind thing to do is to have an automated voice mail system handle the initial calls rather than sending them straight to your office staff. Some of the most popular voice mail systems are <u>Vumber</u>, <u>CallRail</u> and <u>Google Voice</u>. CallRail is a little more expensive, but they have more features including better statistics.

Your answering system is active 24-hours a day. You can prerecord a three to four minute long message that should be designed to further the interest generated by your advertising. Answer common questions, provide more information about the service you advertised or your company. You can even advertise that you have a 24-Hour Hotline.

Make sure that whatever voicemail service you use that it tracks every number that comes in. Every lead should get a follow up – even if they hung up before the message was finished.

Part 3 – Classified Ads

Experienced real estate agents know the value of classified ads. Not only can it generate interest on a specific piece of property, but it will also help to get your business name out there.

Not all classified ads need to be property specific. Have you ever seen those "We by cheap houses" ads? They are quite effective for the demographic they intend to reach. You can do the same thing. Are you looking to list more properties? Consider the following classified ad:

Looking to Sell Your House?
Reduce stress and liability by
hiring a real estate professional.
ABC Realty has 15 years of local experience

Call our 24 Hotline at (333) 333-3333

They call your hotline and get 3 or 4 minute's worth of reasons why hiring a real estate professional is a good move and reasons why your company is the most qualified to help. Whether they leave a number or not, you have theirs.

This type of ad works well both in printed advertising such as newspapers and in online classifieds such as Craigslist.

Part 3 – Targeted Mailing Lists

Bulk mailing to targeted lists is still an effective method of advertising. You list a home in a neighborhood. Why not send a postcard to all the other homes in the neighborhood. Let them know when the open house will be and that they are invited. When you sell the property you should also send out a sold postcard to that same list. If it was a quick sale, guess who they will call when they need to sell.

There are several places online that can provide targeted mailing lists. Here are a few resources for real estate agents: Experian, Listsource, and DMDatabases.com. In addition to these services Click2-Mail will design your advertising media *and* mail them to either your address list or one of their targeted lists.

Another receptive target audience are For Sale by Owners (FSBO). Often they distrust real estate agents or do not want to pay the commission. This gives you a good opportunity to build trust and explain the benefits agents offer to a seller besides simply finding a buyer.

Expired listings are also another targeted opportunity. Tread lightly by waiting for a bit before you start circle the wagons. You do not want to damage your business reputation with your fellow realtors.

Part 4 – Referrals

Referrals are leads with attached personal testimonials. These are extremely effective ways to leap directly from lead to conversion.

Never underestimate the effect of asking for referrals. You can offer an incentive if you want to sweeten the deal. This could be as simple as a $25 gift certificate to a local restaurant for each referral that lists or buys a property through you.

It is a good idea to have your clients complete a customer satisfaction survey after a transaction has been completed. This can create some nice testimonials. At the end of the survey, ask for a referral and offer your carrot incentive.

Generate Leads Through...

Chapter 4 — The Use of Personal Contact

If you really want to make an impact; create a strong business image; and generate concrete leads that convert quickly; then you will need to make personal contact. The most effective advertising campaign is one that combines online, print *and* face-to-face interaction.

As more and more of our surrounding world becomes geared into technology and the instantaneous nature of the internet, there is less and less trust. Buyers are becoming cynical. They suspect that everything is a scam of some sort. This underlying mistrust can create a shaky business relationship from the very start.

How can you combat this trend? You need to build genuine trust. This means that you may need to return to some of the basic real estate techniques that are used by those old-time real estate sages. They know the value of being part of the community. When the community can associate your online and printed advertisements with an actual believable person, they are much more likely to do business with them.

Let's take a few minutes to see how personal contact can turn referrals, leads and contacts into clients.

Part 1 — Open Houses

Sellers expect you to have regular open houses. One of the key benefits of staging an open house is to generate leads. Serious buyers often have their own agents under contract and if their agent is doing their job properly, that buyer will already know about this home and perhaps have even seen it.

Open houses tend to draw the curious and nosy neighbors that have always wanted to see what the inside of the house looked like. They pull out the bored retirees that are looking for something to do. You will also get the potential buyers that are six months to a year out from actually buying. Though few of these will instantly turn into a paying client – they are viable leads.

The nosy neighbor may want to sell in the future – who will they choose to be their agent? Could it be that agent that sold the house across the street that was so friendly when we poked around in the house? Those bored retirees may consider downsizing or purchasing a retirement home in the future. Who will they choose to be their agent? Could it be the one that sends us a monthly State of the Market monthly newsletter? Or how about that couple that is thinking of buying their first home? They haven't chosen an agent but what if you called for a follow up several months down the road?

The key to grooming these leads is to get their contact information before they leave. Remember, consumers are suspicious and skeptical. They think that they do not want to be on a mailing list. They definitely do not want to be hounded. So, you need to develop a method to gain their trust *and* their contact information.

There are several ways that you can obtain follow up information that maximizes your chance of being able to follow up on each and every open house visitor.

Sign-In Sheets
This is perhaps the most obvious way to get contact information and it is a pretty simple way to get it. Having a well-designed display which provides some details about the house and your company set up next to the freshly baked cookies and coffee will catch their attention. Then offer them a free eBook, market report or workbook. All they need to do is sign up and it will be emailed by the end of the day.

Visitors could even select the product they wanted from a list which could include:

- Ten Steps to Sell Your House
- Are Your Ready to Sell? What You Need to Know Before You Start
- Local State of the Market Report
- How to Buy Your First House
- The Top 10 Mistakes Buyers and Sellers Make

Another option is to associate your security measures with a sign-up sheet. You are telling your visitors that you are concerned with the safety and confidentiality of your client - a quality that potential sellers will respect. This can be tactfully handled by having an aid with a clipboard at the door. You will want to have a small disclaimer at the bottom stating that the contact information is for your personal use only and will not be released to third-parties.

The Printed Material

This is a perfect opportunity to make a generous use of your business cards. Or better yet, give all visitors a pen with your contact information. Not only is it a useful gift but they are much more likely to keep it.

Another option is to provide some useful brochures and printouts on topics that would interest the visitors. These can be similar in content to what was discussed above. Make sure that your contact information can be easily seen on each marketing piece.

The Conversation

If you really want to make an impact, create a rapport with each visitor. As they are munching on a cinnamon strudel muffin and sipping that hot apple cider, take a moment to get to know them. Here are some questions that you could ask:

- Are you looking for a house for yourself or someone else?
- How did you find out about the open house?
- Are you working with an agent?
- What do you like about this house?
- What appeals to you about the neighborhood?
- Is there something that you are looking for that this house is lacking?
- Would you like me to see if I could locate a property for you that may work a little better?
- Have you bought a home before?
- Are you pre-qualified for a mortgage?

Be careful, don't interrogate them. Give them their space and be relaxed. Ask questions to get them to open up. Ask them advice on something. Then you can conclude the conversation with something like,

> "I have prepared a helpful guide on (how to buy your first home or how to qualify for a mortgage or a summary of local real estate statistics – pick one). Would you like me to email it to you when I get back to the office? Did you sign-in as you walked in? Okay, no problem, you can write your information down right here and by the way, this pen is yours as a free gift. Help yourself to another cookie and thanks again for coming this afternoon."

Your goal here is to provide a service. Be helpful not pushy. Offer advice not a sales pitch. Look for a way how you could help them down the road by providing more information, advice or pointers. When they leave, they should leave with something from you - either a property printout, a pen, business card, a flyer, brochure, a refrigerator magnet – something that has your contact information on it.

Part 2 — Work Your Farm

As a Realtor, you are going to have a market area that you will want to focus your attention on and become an expert about. Your best clients are going to come from your market area. This is the area you want to farm.

To be a good farmer you are going to need to get out and till up the soil. You could jump on the mass mailing bandwagon and race through the area spending postage to mail a cookie cutter postcard to a nearly nameless house or you could personally go and stir up the soil.

Take the time each week to walk a section of your market area. Knock at the houses and introduce yourself. Though this may seem as scary as becoming a Jehovah's Witness, the method works. It is an excellent way to put a face on your marketing. In fact, let me give you a personal experience.

I recently came back from visiting my parents in Florida. A couple of years ago they bought a foreclosure and retired in the Cape Coral area. One day a real estate agent came knocking. When my mom answered the door, he politely introduced himself and handed her his business card. He said something to the effect of:

> "Good afternoon, I'm _____. What's your name? It is nice to meet you. I am a local real estate agent that specializes in marketing homes in this area. In fact, see that house right there down the road? Yes that's the one. I have it listed and am planning on having an open house this Saturday from 1 to 3 p.m. I wanted to invite you to come and visit. In addition, if you are in the market to upgrade or downsize, I would be more than happy to assist you in that. Again, my name is _____ and I am with _____. My phone number and email address is right here on my business card. Thanks a lot for your time and I hope to see you again on Saturday."

My parents thought that was the neatest thing ever. They mentioned how he was dressed in a tie and seemed so professional. They even said that if they were thinking of selling, they would have gone with him because he took the effort to come to their house to introduce himself. What was their one complaint? They wished he had given them a refrigerator magnet rather than a business card - because they can't seem to find the card.

Part 3 – Attend Real Estate Support Groups

Newbie investors are frequently advised to join a local Real Estate Investors Association (REIA). Nearly every major city has one of these non-profit groups. Have you joined them? You may not be looking for advice, but as an experienced professional you can offer that advice. But the real action happens after the lectures and courses are finished. That is when you can farm for some real solid leads by getting to know who is in attendance. Bring plenty of stamped pens and business cards and be prepared to share them.

Besides networking, participating in a REIA builds your credibility. It can open your eyes to new ideas and local issues. Though you may even contribute your experience as a guest speaker, you too could learn a new technique from time to time.

Part 4 – Participate in Community Events

An excellent way to build trust in your market area is to create the perception that you are not only in real estate to make money but to give back to the community. Keep your eyes open for opportunities for "free" advertising and a chance to get out of the office and into the fresh air.

You can either endorse an activity through contributions or better yet participate in the activity yourself. Help clean the highway. Run in that marathon. Join Big Brothers Big Sisters. But before you leave the house, make sure you have donned your promotional t-shirt and baseball hat. After a Saturday afternoon cleaning the park, imagine what will go through the minds of Mr. and Mrs. Treehugger when they see your face on a yard sign?

Part 5 – Telemarketing the Good Way

I know, we all hate telemarketers. But why do we really hate them? Could it be that they always call at dinner time? Or that they are now computer generated messages that put you on hold? Or perhaps it is the fact that 85% can barely speak English? Probably all of the above.

Telemarketing can be effective – if you do it right. If you want the best response, you need to make the calls. It is that personal interest again. Not farmed out to some cheap overseas company, but personally done by the agent himself. That touch will not go unnoticed.

Next, never call during dinner time. It's just rude. If you call at a different time, say Saturday or Sunday afternoon and no one answers, then leave a message and an easy way to get in touch with you – email or websites are great.

The key to a successful telemarketing campaign, however, is based on the reason for the call. Remember that you are not there to sell them something but to provide some quick information. Try these scripts on for size:

- *"Good afternoon, my name is _____ and I am a local real estate agent with _____. I just wanted to call to let you know that I just listed Mr. _____'s house on _____ Street. I am having an open house on Saturday from 1 to 3 p.m. and I wanted to personally invite you. If you want to check out the house before you come, it is on the home page of my website. Do you have a pen or pencil handy to write it down? It is _____. Thanks so much for your time. Again my name is _____ with _____. I hope to meet you in person on Saturday."*

- *"Good evening, my name is _____ and I am a local real estate agent with _____. I am calling you real quick to give you a heads up on a new listing in your area. Did you know that the _____ house on _____ Road was just listed for sale? If you are curious, I could send you some information about it? Which is better – email or through the post office? Great! I'll post it tomorrow morning. Thanks again for your time. If you are ever in need of a real estate agent or have a friend in need, feel free to give me a call at this number or stop by my website at _____."*

- *"Good morning. My name is _____ and I am a local real estate agent with _____. I am the agent that just sold the house just down the street from you. Because of our aggressive sales techniques and market experience, we were able to beat the odds and sell it in only _____ days. I just wanted to call and see if you or anyone you know is also interested in selling or buying a new home. I offer a free market evaluation package and price opinion with absolutely no obligation. Would you like some information on that? I would be happy to send it over…"*

In each of these scripts, you are calling with information that the homeowner maybe interested in. Because you the agent are calling, you add credibility and personal interest to the phone call. If you really want to nail the presentation, end all of your cold calls asking them what you could do for them.

These are just a few ways that you can create leads through personal contact. As you go through your daily life, keep your eyes and ears open for opportunities to share your real estate wisdom. Look for ways to help out and offer assistance (and then hand them your business card, magnet or pen). People remember the kindness, thoughtfulness and unexpected helpfulness. All which builds trust that leads to commitment.

Chapter 5 – How to Convert Your Leads into Clients

Have you gotten some ideas on how you can generate more leads? We hope so. It is now up to you to take what you have learned and apply it in your business. The more avenues that you focus on, the more leads you will receive.

You may find that some methods are more effective than others. This can be attributed to the time invested, the extent of application and your market area. If you see that some methods yield more results then focus the majority of your attention on that method – but do not give up on the others.

Advertising feeds itself. Just because a potential client responds to one type of advertising does not mean that the other methods were ineffective. It could be the combination of multiple approaches that finally got them to respond to the latest technique.

Leads are great. Leads are necessary. But a lead that does not convert into a client will never put money in your pocket. So now that you have the leads, how to you convert them into paying customers? This is the end game. If you drop the ball here, then your business is going to struggle to grow and you will be spending much and reaping little.

Use Software to Manage Your Leads

No doubt you have seen the agents that live in perpetual panic. Their desk is cluttered with little scraps of paper, each with a name, phone number and or appointment date. The dash of their car is covered in

Post-it notes. In reality, they are just hoping that they remember everything because they will never find that scrap of paper in time.

Now I am not saying that you cannot have a manually written ledger of your leads. If you are reluctant to step over into the 21st Century, I can understand that. I am not sure how well you will do in an industry that is racing to adapt everything technology – but if you like paper, then go for it.

I don't really care what type of system you use, just make sure you have an *organized* system of recording, tracking and following up on every single lead – every phone call, every voicemail, every email, referral, business card... every handshake. There are a lot of really good tools out there to help you keep track of this. A good customer relationship management software package will save you so much time that it will quickly pay for itself and allow you to focus on serving your clients rather than chasing them.

Customer relationship management software is also known as CRM. Think of it as your seller lead database. Though the following list is just an overview of what is available, it will give you an idea of what can be done and some of the leading software that does it.

> Zoho CRM – *(Free or CRMPlus for $50 Month/User.)* This is a well-designed customizable system. Their system communicates with leads via email, phone, chat and social media. It works with Google Apps and has a strong scheduler app as well.
>
> In summing up their opinion of this software, PC Magazine said, "Zoho CRM isn't much to look at, but its drab interface offers plenty of sales, email marketing, reporting and customer service power for small and medium-sized businesses, at an affordable price."
>
> Highrise – *($24 - $149/month.)* This software is advertised as a "Simple CRM software tool that helps you stay organized." It is just that. It has a limited set of basic contact management

features without all the unnecessary, and often distracting, bells and whistles.

Realeflow – ($29 - $99/month.) This software is geared toward the real estate wholesaler and flipper. You can daily import real estate leads from their database. It can automate your emails and direct mail campaigns and even setup multiple websites. It has a deal analyzer side to the software as well and can manage a fix-and-flip all the way to the sales side of things.

FreedomSoft – (30 Days Free, $97 - $297/Month) Here is another program that has been designed specifically for the real estate market with a focus on flippers. It is a little softer in the CRM section than Realeflow. But, it nearly automates the whole process including lead databases, email campaigns, website creation and even auto-fill contracts.

REI BlackBook – (Free Trial, $997 plus $97/Month) This pricey CRM package is well designed and focuses on the needs of real estate agents. It publishes websites, manages leads, automates marketing and analyzes deals for those focusing on wholesaling and property flipping.

Top Producer CRM – ($39.95 - $84.95/Month) This software has been around for a long time and has been designed for the real estate market. It can track a transaction from lead to close and also integrates with other lead management sources. This is the software of choice for many real estate agents. It focuses on automated personalized lead follow-up.

Salesforce – ($60 to $125 per month/user.) This software has been around for a long time and pretty much invented cloud-based CRM. They offer sales, marketing and service management capabilities.

Here is what PC Magazine had to say about this software, "If you're willing to pay top dollar, Salesforce.com gives SMBs a mature, robust, highly customizable CRM platform that's second to none in performance."

Podio - *Free (Up to 5 Users), $9.00, $14 and $24 Month per User.* This software is completely customizable to fit your particular needs. It can be designed to manage your entire business - not just the lead management side of things - across multiple platforms. You can pick and choose the features you need and use. It also works seamlessly with the most common file-sharing services like Google Docs, DropBox and OneNote.

Here is what PC Magazine said was their bottom line, "The online-based Podio straddles two lines, online project management and business social network, with alacrity. It's one of the most comprehensive tools for small business communication and work management you'll find."

Each of these systems will have its strengths and its weaknesses. Before you decide which to use, take into consideration your own strengths and weaknesses. If you already have a great website, do you need software that offers that? Try to focus on the system that you really need: lead follow-up.

The most common gap in lead generation is not necessarily getting the leads but developing the leads into someone that will call you when they need real estate assistance. This means that you need to print your name, face and business identity in their mind. That will only happen through repeated contact. Look for CRM software that will automate that step of the business system for you.

Create a System

Once you choose a customer relation management software package, now you need to create a system to maximize its potential. Every lead that comes in should have a next action assigned to it. As you enter the lead into your software, take the time right then and there to decide *what* the next action is and *when* that action will happen.

Different leads will have different actions and response times. If it is a phone lead, why did they call you? Do they want to sell their house?

Are they in need of an agent now or in the future? Did you say you would get back to them by a certain date? All of this should be entered into the CRM. If you want to really get things automated, link your CRM (like Podio) to your voicemail and your website. If someone signs up on the website, it would automatically get put into the CRM.

It is a good idea to take a few minutes and physically write down how you want to handle your leads. There should be a step-by-step list for website responses, voicemails, referrals etc. Then, design the response or follow-up each lead will receive. If they need a callback, create the script. If you plan to send them an instructional email with a link to a video, then type it up with a blank space for their name. I think you get the idea, right? In this way, not only will each lead get handled in the same way, but you can then outsource your lead management to a virtual assistant or office staff.

Get a VA to Help

Time is an enemy to lead generation. As your business grows, it can be easy to shove lead generation aside and focus on the project at hand. The problem with that time management choice is that eventually the project will end and you will not have any leads to shake out a new client.

An easy way around this conundrum is to outsource your lead management to a virtual assistant or staff member. They will be your front line. It will give you time to focus on your actual clients and making the actual money. Now do you see why it is important to create a lead follow-up to-do list? Now you not only have your leads automatically generated through targeted advertising but you have the follow-up automated as well.

Now you not only have your leads automatically generated through targeted advertising but you have the follow-up au-

You can hire local staff to help you with this. If you have a secretary with free time on their hands, they can be quickly integrated into this task. If you want to reduce costs, however, consider employing a virtual assistant. You can locate highly skilled virtual assistants off the web through an outsourcing site such as UpWork or Virtual Staff Finder. There are varying degrees of skill and pay depending on the tasks you would like them to handle for you. The better you have created your systems, the better a VA can work to convert your leads.

Chapter 6 – 10 Tips to Effectively Generate Leads

When it is all said and done, effective lead generation needs to be focused on what you can do to help and assist your potential clients and customers. If your main goal is simply to drum up business, then you are going to come off as a used car salesman trying to meet his end of the month quota.

Of course, a business will not last long if you do not work to drive the public to your service or product. But if that is your primary motivation, your potential clients will see that and be turned off.

How can you steer clear of the "I need money. Buy from me" mentality? Try not to focus on making money and convincing customers to do business with you. Instead, look to see what you can do to serve your potential customers. Prove to them that you are an expert in your field and that you are there to help them. That higher level of personal service makes all the difference. It creates a loyalty that overshadows price.

When you turn the attention off making money at all costs and turn the spotlight on your contacts and clients, not only will your customers appreciate it but you will feel less stress as well. You will also be surprised about how the money quietly finds its way into your bank account.

Look to see what you can do to serve your potential customers.

If you want to take lead generation to a whole new level, then work hard to apply these ten tips.

Tip #1 - Create a System to Generate Leads

We all know that if we want to be healthy then we need to exercise. It is a known fact… but just knowing we need exercise is not enough to get us going to the gym. Good health does not happen by accident. Time needs to be scheduled for it and then you have to get up and work out.

The same is true with lead generation. We all know we need to do it. But only thinking about the need will not accomplish much. You need to sit down and devise a system to generate the leads. We have discussed a lot of different tactics in this publication. Pick the ones that you think will be the most effective and will bring the best results. Now design an action plan and a schedule to accomplish it. Spending just 15 minutes a day following up on your lead generating system will yield exceptional results.

Tip #2 – Do Not Annoy Potential Clients

Effective lead generation techniques include regular communication with your contacts. Regular contact, however, does not mean that you stalk them. They do not want to receive daily, or even weekly, emails from you. Make regular contact by using various methods. Remember to contact them with something of value rather than an in-your-face company promotion.

Tip #3 – Provide a Product or Service in Exchange for a Lead

This is the perfect example of the proverb, "You scratch my back and I'll scratch yours." If you give a potential customer something of value, they can express appreciation by giving a referral. You can also ask for an email address in order to email them a valuable eBook. Invite your website visitors to sign-up for a helpful webinar. All of these methods are non-invasive ways to generate a lead. The key is to offer something of genuine value.

Tip #4 – Generate Leads Everyday

When you design your lead generating system, it should be able to provide you with solid leads each and every day – we are not talking about the *potential* for leads but actual concrete pursuable leads. If your website is not drawing in several leads each day, then perhaps it is time to revamp the site or market it harder.

In addition to static advertising which would include Craigslist ads, websites, classifieds and yard signs, look to add dynamic advertising each and every day. This is contact that is personally made. It can be as simple as handing out a business card (or better yet a refrigerator magnet or pen). Asking for referrals is another effective way to daily generate leads.

Tip #5 – Follow up on Each and Every Lead

Two missed calls and three hang-ups but no voice messages. Return the missed calls as soon as absolutely possible. These are clients or leads that are calling for a specific reason.

What about the hang-ups? They may not have made it all the way through your voicemail presentation, but they called. They made the first step. It is still a lead and every phone number should be followed up no matter how small the lead. It can grow with time and patience. Never let a lead fall through the cracks – never.

Tip #6 – Maximize Your Leads through Customer Relationship Management (CRM) Software

One way to help your leads from getting misplaced and forgotten is to use CRM software. Not only is it a database to handle each lead and current client, but it can also automate your follow-up system. When CRM software is linked to an email and phone system, following up on leads becomes almost second nature.

Tip #7 – Build an Online Presence with Local Residents

People are turning more and more to the internet to find guidance, advice and answers to their questions – all well before they make physical contact with a local professional. You can easily generate leads by being the expert that is there online to answer their question. They will quickly associate your online help with your local business. Once trust is established, a business partnership is much easier to create.

Tip #8 – Generate Leads by Giving Back to the Community

You want your name out there. You want people in the community to know who you are, what you do and how to contact you. If you want that, then you cannot be a hermit living in some remote office. You need to be in the public's eye and what a better way to do that then to don your company t-shirt and participate in community activities. (Don't forget to bring some pens and magnets as well... just in case you make first contact.)

Tip #9 – Do not Forget to Use Direct Mail Marketing

Online marketing is popular, but that is not to say that direct mail is dead. In fact, online marketing has dramatically reduced the amount of junk mail. This opens an opportunity to get the word out (and be seen) that you offer services that can benefit them. You do not need to come off hard or pushy. A postcard featuring a local open house or a nearby property sale can be just the nudge a seller needs to pick up the phone.

Tip #10 – Stick to Your System

Lead generation will not work well unless it is a long-term activity. It is not an item on a to-do list that once you have completed it you no longer have to think about it. Instead, this should be part of your business activity – just like returning phone calls, paying bills and ordering office supplies is a regular part of your day-to-day activities. The longer a system is active (though refined and tweaked now and again) the better it will function.

Well there you have it. The main ways to generate leads using the Internet, advertising media and personal contact. If you generate a lead system that uses the best out of all three categories simultaneously, you may very well find out that you will need extra staff just to handle the increased business.

Keep your focus on your client and not on earning money. Provide them a service. Offer them your skills. Share news and advice and you will find that lead generation becomes a money making social activity and less like work.

Could I ask a huge favor of you? Could you take 30 seconds to leave a review on Amazon? I would be forever grateful.

More books by Brent Driscoll:

Wholesaling Real Estate: A Beginners Guide

Becoming a Real Estate Agent: A Comprehensive Guide on How to Become a Real Estate Agent

Flipping Houses for Profit: A Comprehensive Guide on How to Flip Houses for Maximum ROI

Rental Property Investing for the Rest of Us: The Beginners Guide to Successful Rental Property Investing

Made in the USA
Middletown, DE
30 July 2021